T0077749

A Reason To Believe

The Wonder Of It All

BONNIE CARAWAY BROWN

A G.R.A.C.E. WORKS! PRODUCTION

BALBOA.
PRESS

A DIVISION OF HAY HOUSE

Balboa Press books may be ordered through booksellers or by contacting:

Balboa Press
A Division of Hay House
1663 Liberty Drive
Bloomington, IN 47403
www.balboapress.com
1-(877) 407-4847

ISBN: 978-1-4525-3250-9 (sc)
ISBN: 978-1-4525-3256-1 (e)

Printed in the United States of America

Balboa Press rev. date: 3/28/2011

Wonder

Definition: Wonder

Wonder

Noun

1. The feeling aroused by something strange and surprising.
2. Something that causes feelings of wonder; "the wonders of modern science".
3. A state in which you want to learn more about something.

Verb

1. Have a wish or desire to know something; "He wondered who had built this beautiful church".
2. Place in doubt or express doubtful speculation; "I wonder whether this was the right thing to do"; "she wondered whether it would snow tonight".
3. Be amazed at; "We marveled at the child's linguistic abilities".
   Source: <u>WordNet 1.7.1</u> Copyright © 2001 by Princeton University. All rights reserved.

Contents

1. The Beginning   1
2. Joy   5
3. Best Friends   9
4. Law of Physics   11
5. Shopping   13
6. Skateboarding   15
7. More foreshadowing?   17
8. Broken Leg   21
9. A Visit?   23
10. "MOM!"   25
11. Playing With The Lights   29
12. Coincidences?   31
13. Out Of The Mouth of Babes   33
14. Psychic Connection   35
15. OHM   41
16. If I Could Find That Dime   45

Foreword

What is of greatest importance in a person's life is not just the nature and extent of his or her experiences but what has been learned from them.

---Norman Cousins

I have learned that death is not the enemy. We are all dying from the moment we enter this world. For some of us the stay here is a lengthy one. For others, it's much briefer. But no matter what amount of time is allotted to us in this life, one thing is certain. Our physical bodies were not meant to live forever. God deliberately designed the human body to end at some point. He does not make mistakes. So when a person dies, whether after having lived a long and meaningful life or after only being on this Earth for a few days or even a few minutes, that is the way that particular life was supposed to be. Death is very much a natural part of life and, if we will just be open to it, it can be a great teacher and soul advancer.

I have learned that the more you look for the positives in life, the easier they are to see. Even in the face of great adversity, such as the death of a child, there are positives. Don't get me wrong. I'm not a "Pollyanna", always seeing the best life has to offer and trying to avoid the harsh realities that go hand in hand with them. No, I struggled horribly after the death of my son. Grief and depression were my constant companions at first. The grief was so consuming I thought it would swallow me whole. But it didn't. Instead, it left me broken and depressed. I gradually began to realize that I was going to have to deal with the pain, stay in this world and somehow learn to live again. Live even though it seemed my life would never be whole again. But I did learn to live again. And I learned to see the positives in situations where before I thought there were none. I learned to listen for and hear God's wonders where before I would have missed them. My hope is that in reading this book and hearing about my journey, your journey and your path will be lightened and you too, will find the wonders in life which give you a reason to believe.

Acknowledgements

Thank you to my wonderful family who supported me through my grief even while they were dealing with their own. For they all loved and were loved by Cody:

My son, Matt

My daughter, Marisa

My sister, Joni

And

My parents, Bob & Barbara Caraway

My nephew, James

My Aunt and Cody's Great-Aunt Mary Anne

Cody's father, Charley

I want to extend my heartfelt gratitude to each and every person who attended Cody's viewing and funeral. There were far too many of you for me to be able to thank personally. So, on the slight chance that you are reading this book because you know me or knew Cody and attended his funeral, thank you from the bottom of my heart. Your presence helped ease our pain even though it may not have appeared so at the time.

The Beginning

My youngest child, Cody was 16 years old when he left this world. Did he choose to leave or was it just an accident? Is anything ever really an accident? Do we make choices on a deeper level that our conscious minds aren't aware of? Do we know things on a deeper level? Is this knowledge always present within our subconscious or soul?

I wonder.

Even though it happened over six years ago now, I can remember that February day as if it were just yesterday. I had driven Cody over to his best friend Daniel's house so he could ride to school with Daniel and his younger sister. Daniel had gotten his driver's license the previous November and had been driving himself back and forth to school for several months prior to being allowed to have anyone else ride with him. The next step was for Stacy, his younger sister to ride with him for a few weeks and then Cody was allowed to ride as well. The kids had all grown up together, having lived on the same block in the same neighborhood since the boys were two years old. I had two other children, Matt who was 22 and Marisa who was 19 and I had not allowed either of them to ride with a friend so soon after getting a driver's license, so why did I let Cody? I don't know except that Cody had a difficult time fitting in from the time he left elementary school and started middle school. The difficulties stayed with him right on into high school. Riding to school with a friend made him feel like he fit in more so I gave in. Daniel's family had recently moved off the block where the kids had all grown up so I would drive Cody over to Daniel's in the morning and pick him up from there in the afternoons. Little did I know that the hurried kiss and "I love you" as he bolted from the car and disappeared into Daniel's backyard were the last I would ever get from him. If I hadn't let him ride with Daniel that day would it have made a difference? Would he still be alive or would a different type of accident still have claimed his life?

I wonder.

I worked from home at the time so I was sitting at my computer working that afternoon when I started to realize that it was past time for Cody to call me from Daniel's to come and pick him up. I called Daniel's mom Alba to see if she had heard from the kids. She hadn't but neither one of us was too concerned at that point as it was only a few minutes since school had let out. I decided to drive over to my parent's house which was just around the block from Daniel's to wait for the boys. I told Alba to have Cody call me there when they got home. Soon after, I was sitting in my mother's kitchen talking with her when the phone rang and I heard Alba's voice on the other end telling me to come quickly. "They've had an accident, he's hurt but he's all right". I took off out of the house telling my mother to stay by the phone and I'd call her as soon as I knew anything.

I arrived at the accident site just after the ambulance. The paramedics were already working on the kids. It was obvious that the car had flipped, the roof was caved in and there was broken glass everywhere. There was no other car involved. The kids all seemed to be fairly okay except for Cody. Daniel was standing up, his pants legs were torn and ripped and he seemed to be in a daze. Stacy was sitting on the side of the road yelling in pain not to touch her as one of the paramedics was putting a neck brace on her. There were two other teens there who had obviously been in the accident but who were relatively untouched. Cody was lying on the roadside, unconscious with his left arm "de-gloved" which means the entire outer layer of skin had been cut and pulled down, similar to pulling a glove off your hand. I remember thinking "Dear God, don't let him lose his arm. All he ever wanted was to be normal and fit in with the other kids. Please don't let him lose his arm; I don't think he can handle that". Little did I know that his arm wasn't the worst of his injuries. I kept telling him that I was there and that everything was going to be okay. The paramedics finally got him on the stretcher and into the ambulance and I followed them to the hospital. We were able to get all the other family members to the hospital before the doctor who examined Cody came out to tell us the news. Cody had suffered massive brain damage in the accident. The doctor didn't think he would make it through surgery. He did make it through the surgery but the neurosurgeon who worked on him came out to us following the surgery to report that the damage was even more extensive than he had previously thought. The following days showed even more brain swelling and the x-rays showed more dead brain cells. Cody's father and I made the decision to take Cody off of life support two and a half days after the accident. He died about twenty minutes later. And now this is where the real story begins.

Joy

The other accident victims had been taken to a different hospital from the one Cody had been taken to. Both of the other boys had been treated and released. The girls were held overnight for observation and then released. At the hospital where we were, countless friends, neighbors and classmates filled the waiting room and helped us keep a vigil for Cody. Needless to say, I was distraught and operating on sheer nerves during the 2 ½ - day hospital stay. There were many people who hugged me, said comforting words to me or just cried with me. I can't remember them all. However, one thing or should I say three things, stand out in my mind about that time at the hospital. First though, let me tell you about our morning the day of the accident.

Cody had begun having anxiety and panic attacks around the second half of sixth grade which was the beginning of middle school. These attacks became bad enough and disabling enough that he had to be home schooled for the second half of sixth grade and for several years thereafter. Eventually we were able to get his anxiety and panic attacks under control and Cody returned to school in his freshman year of high school. But even then, the anxiety was just under the surface and he would look for any opportunity to miss a day and stay home. This was especially so on school "half-days". Our school system has teacher planning days once every nine weeks. On these days, the students are let out early, just after lunch. Well, Cody would always beg me to let him stay home on "half-days" telling me they really didn't do any work. They just watched movies or had study hall so he really wouldn't be missing anything if he didn't go. He would start the begging and wheedling the night before and continue it immediately upon waking the next morning. He would say things like, "I bet Daniel's not going. If Daniel doesn't go, can I stay home, too? Please mom, c'mon, I'll be your best friend". I always dreaded the "half-days" because I knew the struggle was coming. I'll admit, sometimes I gave in and let him stay home. But there was no struggle on this "half-day" morning. No, this morning he was up as soon as his alarm clock went off. I remember he was in an exceptionally good mood and was joking around with me. He never said anything about not going to school. In retrospect, I should have realized this was not an ordinary day. But on that day, I was just relieved he hadn't begged to stay home and thought maybe he was outgrowing his anxieties or at least, coming to terms with them.

When he started high school he was obsessed with fitting in and being normal. I know that fitting in is the goal for all teens at this age but for Cody, having missed most of middle school with his classmates, it was even more important in his mind for him to fit in. I found out that the reason they were late getting home from school on that last day was because of Cody. It seems that he was out in the parking lot goofing off with some friends, making jokes, laughing and looking forward to the weekend. He was fitting in.

Now, for the thing that stands out in my mind about that day, Cody's last day of living in this world and his first day in the hospital. Two of Cody's teachers and his guidance counselor all came up to me at the hospital and said virtually the same thing, all unbeknownst to each other and all at different times. Each one told me that she had seen Cody at school that day and that he had joy on his face. That was the term each of them used. He had "Joy on his face". Not that he was happy or that he was in a good mood, or a silly mood. Three times I was told he had "Joy on his face".

When you take these seemingly innocent and unrelated incidences, the fact that he didn't beg to stay home and miss school on this "half-day" but actually seemed to be looking forward to it, his classmates telling me about his goofing off in the parking lot prior to coming home and his teachers and counselor telling me about their last encounters with him earlier in the morning, it makes me wonder. My son was happy, he was fitting in and there was Joy on his face. Even though it was only for a few short hours, he was finally living the life he longed for. Did Cody know on a soul level that his journey here was coming to an end? Did his soul know he was truly going home?

I wonder.

Best Friends

Cody died in the spring of 2002 as a result of the injuries he suffered in an accident involving his best friend. In the fall of 2001, my childhood best friend moved back to town after having lived in Texas for twenty-something years. Brenda and I had kept in touch sporadically. She would come to town to visit her parents who still lived here and we would try to get together. Or we'd call each other every now and then, but we didn't remain as close as either one of us thought we would. You know how it is, we all have good intentions but then life gets in the way. For us though, death also got in the way, and brought us back together. We were still bound by a bond that had been forged from sharing a childhood. From elementary school through high school and everything in between, we were inseparable. There was complete trust between us that can only come from sharing each other's highest highs and lowest lows. While she had been in Texas, my friend lost her dear mother to cancer. Throughout her mother's battle with the disease, Brenda tried every type of resource she could get her hands on to help her mother. This included alternative medicines and metaphysical healings. Her research into these fields brought to her a different mindset, a different way of seeing things. Once she came home, she began telling me bits and pieces of her new beliefs and the whole new world that had opened up for her once she started studying the metaphysical world. Even though these were new concepts to me, I had been raised Catholic and never really questioned my faith, I knew Brenda to be a rational and intelligent woman. She was also a dear friend whom I would trust with my life. So I listened and I began to learn.

Did Brenda come home to Pensacola after her divorce because she wanted to leave the pain and memories of a failed marriage behind in Texas? Or did God bring her home because He knew I would trust her and He intended to use her as a tool to help me put my life back together?

I wonder.

Law of Physics

After Cody's death I was distraught at the thought of having lost him forever. According to the laws of physics, energy is constant. Therefore, while our physical bodies can die and cease to exist, our souls or the energy that fuels our bodies does not. I now became as obsessed with finding where Cody or his soul was, as Cody had been about fitting in and being normal. As it turns out, I didn't have far to look. At Cody's viewing and funeral service there was standing room only. He would have loved to have been there to see how many people turned out to say good-bye to him and to tell stories about how his life had touched theirs. I had gone into what I think was a break room at the funeral home that night with Brenda and another friend just to sit and catch my breath before going back out and visiting with everyone. As we sat there, the lights flickered off and on. Brenda chuckled and said, "Cody's here". It wasn't a stormy night. There was no reason for the lights to flicker. I suppose it could have been a problem in the wiring. But, could it have been Cody letting us know of his presence? Was he aware of my despair and was he letting me know that he was still with me? Or better still, was he trying to let me know how much he was enjoying all the attention he was getting?

I wonder.

Shopping

My mother used to take Cody grocery shopping with her. While I had to make him go with me griping and complaining the whole way, he gladly went with Grandmom. In fact, every time he'd see her he'd ask, "Don't you need anything from the grocery store, Grandmom"? That's because she would buy him a WWF wrestling magazine each time they went. He knew I considered them a waste of money and there was no way he was getting one out of me! To encourage (or bribe) him to go with her, Grandmom would always buy him a wrestling magazine as a reward for going to the store and helping her with the groceries. I'll never forget the first day I was able to go back to the grocery store after his death. I was with my sister, Joni. We were standing in the check-out line waiting our turn when I suddenly felt something hit me in the back and drop to the floor. I turned around expecting to see someone behind me who might have dropped something but there was no one there. I looked down and saw a magazine lying face down on the floor. I turned it over and, you guessed it, looking back at me was the cover of a WWF Wrestling magazine. Okay, coincidence you might say. I accidentally knocked a magazine off the shelf and didn't realize it. Could be, except that the check-out lane we were in didn't have any magazines displayed nor did they have a shelf for one to be lying on for me to accidentally knock down. A hello from Cody letting me know he was still with me?

I wonder.

Skateboarding

As I said earlier, Cody's fatal automobile accident happened in February. The previous August he broke his leg in a skateboarding accident. After much begging and pleading on his part, I agreed to let him go to a newly opened skateboard park on the condition that Charley, his dad, would go with him. Shortly after they got to the park, Cody decided to try and land a jump off a ten foot ramp. By the way, Cody wasn't the most graceful skateboarder you'd ever want to see. Needless to say, he didn't land the jump correctly. He broke both the tibia and fibula in his left leg. His dad rushed him to Baptist Hospital and called me to meet them there. The doctors at Baptist Hospital felt sure Cody would need surgery but wanted a pediatric orthopedic surgeon's opinion. Since Baptist Hospital didn't have one on staff, that meant Cody would have to be seen across town at Sacred Heart Hospital. Because he was hooked up to IV pain medication and to avoid as much jostling around as possible, Cody made the trip from Baptist to Sacred Heart by ambulance. His dad and I each had our own cars so we followed the ambulance separately. Now, I know by this time that my son is going to be okay. Actually, he wasn't in any pain anymore because of the morphine they were pumping into him. I had seen him, talked to him, kissed and hugged him and heard him assure me he was all right. So how do I explain the near panic and rising fear that I was fighting with during the entire ride from one hospital to the other? When Charley had called me saying that Cody had broken his leg and to meet them at the hospital, I wasn't overly concerned. Charley was with him and he was taking care of things. Still, I hadn't seen or talked to Cody to make sure for myself that he was okay. Wouldn't it have made more sense for me to be panicky and scared then? Instead, I almost lost it during that ten minute ride behind the ambulance from one hospital to the other when I knew my son was okay.

Could that ride behind an ambulance carrying my injured son have been a foreshadowing of things to come? It is said that we have all the answers we need within ourselves, deep in our souls. Did my soul have knowledge of that fatal accident still to come? An accident which would also have me driving behind an ambulance carrying my injured son to a hospital. And did my conscious mind somehow communicate with my soul and pick up a small part of that knowledge and misinterpret it? Did the panic and fear I was feeling that August night really belong to a cold February day yet to come?

I wonder.

More foreshadowing?

Let me tell you about two other incidents I experienced prior to Cody's death. The first thing that happened to me didn't directly involve Cody. He was with me but it actually involved my daughter, Marisa. Marisa had been hired as a riding counselor at a summer camp the summer before Cody's accident. The camp was in Lakeland, FL which is about 800 miles from where we live in Pensacola, FL. I was glad she had gotten the opportunity but I wasn't happy about her driving down there by herself. The closest airport to the ranch was in Orlando which was still a good hour's drive away and since the ranch wasn't equipped to provide transportation to and from the airport for their summer employees, she would still have to arrange transportation from the airport out to the ranch. In the end, I decided that the three of us, Marisa, Cody and I would take a few days and drive her down there and do a little sightseeing on the way. As it turned out, the closer we got to the ranch, the more nervous and excited Marisa was to start her summer adventure. We decided to just drive straight on to the ranch, get her settled and then Cody and I would do the sightseeing on our way back home. Things didn't work out that way after all. We had all been in a good mood, laughing and enjoying being together when we pulled up to the gate that announced we had reached the ranch. Things were still okay as we unpacked Marisa's things from the car and met with the head camp counselor. We were shown to Marisa's cabin and got her situated and began to say our goodbyes. This is where things got strange. As Cody and I got into the car and headed back down the dirt road that led to the highway, a strange sense of sadness and dread came over me. I remember starting to cry and trying to hide it so Cody wouldn't notice. A few minutes later when I could no longer control the tears, and had to just let them pour down at will, Cody asked me why I was crying. "Oh, I'm just being a mom", I said. To that he replied, in typical little brother fashion, "Mom, we're just leaving her here for six weeks. You should be happy for the peace and quiet we're going to have. I know I am!" I know you're probably thinking there's nothing unusual about a mother crying as she leaves her child at summer camp. But my child was 19 years old and this wasn't her first time away from home. And besides, I remember not understanding the depth of my sadness myself. To this day I can remember how I felt and it's not unlike the way I felt following the ambulance after Cody's skateboarding accident a few months later.

The second incident is even more benign. Yet, it is because of this that it makes me wonder even more. Cody had been begging me to go see the movie, The Lord of the Rings. This was not my type of movie and I did not want to go sit through it. His older brother Matt would have taken him but he had already seen it, as had most of Cody's friends. So of course, I went to the movie with him. To my surprise, I found myself enjoying the movie. More than that, I was entranced by it. Now remember, I said this was not my type of movie. I didn't know the first thing about the story line. I hadn't paid any attention to the ads nor had I read the book. Had I paid attention, I might have known that the movie was going to end with a lot of unanswered questions. That's what happens when there are going to be sequels to the movie. As it was though, I was completely unprepared for the movie's abrupt ending. As with the summer camp incident, my reaction to the movie's ending was completely out of character. I ranted on and on for weeks afterwards that I couldn't believe the movie had ended so suddenly. Again, I was filled with an overwhelming sense of sadness and despair whenever I thought about it. It actually shook me up to the point that I remember my mother even commenting on my reaction. To this day it still doesn't make any sense. Or does it?

With both of these incidents, was my soul trying to tell me something again? And in the telling from soul to consciousness did the message get confused? Did my soul know that I would be telling Cody good-bye in this life and did my conscious mind misinterpret the summer good-bye I said to Marisa at the ranch for that one? Even though Cody was on life support for 2 ½ days, I have always felt his life ended abruptly at the accident scene, at the moment of impact. He was unconscious when I arrived at the scene and he never regained consciousness. Did the movie's abrupt ending resonant with my soul's knowledge that Cody's life was coming to an abrupt end and did my conscious mind not know how to interpret the message?

I wonder.

Broken Leg

One evening several months after Cody's death Brenda called to ask me to go visit a psychic with her. Brenda was putting together a large metaphysical expo later on in the summer and she had heard of a local psychic named Sharon Renae who might be interested in participating in the expo. Sharon Renae lived in Navarre, a small neighboring town about twenty minutes down the highway. On Friday evenings she would open her home to small groups of people who wanted to try and "connect to the other side". I had never had any interest in the psychic world nor believed in it very much prior to Cody's death. But, as I've said before, I don't believe our energy ceases to exist at our physical death and I was open to anyone and anything that might help me understand more about where my Cody was.

Still, I was skeptical about the whole thing and went into it thinking that at least it would get me out of the house. I was fighting depression and knew that being around people would be a good thing. So, I agreed to go with Brenda and see what Sharon Renae was all about. My sister and my aunt came with us, too.

Sharon's house was no different than any other house in the neighborhood and she was no different than any other woman you might see in the grocery store or mall. She was an attractive, blond petite woman with a warm smile and a hug for everyone. There were about twelve to fifteen people at Sharon's that night and she invited us all to sit around her living room in chairs that she had gathered in a circle. Sharon began the reading by thanking us all for coming and reciting a prayer. Everything she does is very God-based and she lets you know that up front. If you've ever watched John Edward's show "Crossing Over", that is much what Sharon's readings are like.

She got a few messages for several people in the room and I have to admit, I wasn't paying much attention. I did hold my hand up though when she asked, actually it was more of a questioning statement, "Somebody here had a loved one pass over recently?" There were several others in the room with their hands up. Of course there would be, why else would all of us be there? Then when Sharon said, "I'm getting a male energy", mine was the only hand left raised. She came over to stand in front of me and said that she was not good at getting names but what she was hearing sounded like "Toby". Well, that's close to Cody but I merely shook my head in the affirmative and allowed her to continue. She went on to say that the energy she was receiving was communicating a broken leg to her. My skepticism was out in full force. I shook my head "no" the whole time thinking to myself, "He had two broken wrists, broken ribs and massive head trauma but no broken leg". She kept saying that he was insisting on having a broken leg and I kept insisting he didn't! She had just given up and said maybe the message wasn't for me when my sister elbowed me in the ribs and whispered "remember, back in August"? Then the light bulb went on; the skateboarding accident! "Yes, yes", I said, "he did have a broken leg". I had been so consumed with memories of the fatal automobile accident that took him from me that I had totally forgotten about anything else. Sharon visibly sighed in relief and said, "Thank you, he was insisting he had a broken leg. He also said to tell you he doesn't limp anymore." That's what really got me. There's no way she could have known that because of the break occurring where it did, with both the tibia and fibula being broken and a growth plate being involved, the orthopedic surgeon had told us Cody would more than likely have a permanent limp! The kids at school had nicknamed him Gimp.

I'm still a skeptic and probably will be until the day I die. But could Sharon Renae have been communicating with Cody's energy? Was it really him giving her this information to relay back to me? Was he there in the room with me and I just couldn't see or hear him?

I wonder.

22

A Visit?

Early one morning about six months after Cody's death I had a dream that I'm not so sure was just a dream. If you've ever read any accounts of near death experiences (NDE's) you know that a common thread among them is an indescribable feeling of love and peace. This experience brought me just such a feeling. Now don't get me wrong, I'm not trying to say this was an NDE. I was very much alive when this happened to me. Sure, it happened during a time when I didn't really *want* to be alive, but I was. I honestly don't know what this experience was. I've quit trying to figure it out. I just accept it as a gift and treasure the memory of it.

After Cody's death, I couldn't bear to be in the house alone. My other two children had moved out prior to Cody's death. They both told me it was too hard for them to come by because they still half expected to find Cody there. So I sold the house and my daughter and I, along with my sister who had also sold her house, moved in with my parents for awhile. My sister is like a second mom to all of my children, she is extremely close to all of them. We all came together as a family and we found comfort and healing in each other. It was there, at my parent's house that I had the dream/experience. In the dream, I was standing in the kitchen of my old house. Cody was there, dressed just like he had been when I dropped him off at Daniel's house that fateful morning. The last glimpse I had of him before seeing him at the accident scene was of his back as he went through the gate in Daniel's fence to go in the back door of the house. He had on jeans with his green skateboard sweatshirt with the hood up and his backpack on his back. This is how he appeared in the dream. He had on those same clothes. The strange thing is that his back was facing me throughout the dream. It was just like I had seen him last. We communicated as if by mental telepathy. There were no words spoken but we both knew what the other was saying. Cody was telling me that he was okay. I remember being happy that he was there and hearing that he was doing okay. But on top of that, I was feeling a peace that I can't put into words. I remember Cody telling me had had to go and hearing my dog barking in the other room. I knew that I was waking up and leaving this wonderful feeling. What strikes me as strange is that, despite how much I love Cody and how much I loved being in his presence again, I wasn't concerned that he was leaving. I knew he would be okay. But I did not want that wonderful feeling of love and peacefulness to leave me. Of all the experiences I have had since Cody's death, this one has been the one that brought me the most intense feeling. As I said before, there is no way for me to define or describe the joy, peace and feeling of utter contentment I felt that morning. It couldn't have been an NDE. Even though that was during the time when I would have welcomed death, I wasn't anywhere near death. If it was a dream, it was like none other I've ever had, before or since. Could it have been a visit from Cody's soul to mine? I'll never know, at least not in this life. But,

I wonder.

"MOM!"

About a year after Cody's death when some healing had begun to take place, my sister and I decided to buy a house together. My daughter and a friend of hers were also going to live with us there. We had the house built and watched it take shape over the space of about 10 months. We moved in during the spring and were really enjoying the house. The first Christmas in the house was our second one without Cody. While building and moving had kept me occupied, nothing ever really took my mind off of Cody for long. It was early on in that second Christmas season that I had the most unusual experience; and my sister was there to share it with me.

It actually started one summer night after moving into the new house. I was in bed, in that wonderfully delicious state between wakefulness and sleep where you just seem to float along weightlessly, I was roused just a bit by the sound of Cody calling, "Mom!". It sounded like he was way off in the distance and at about the same time it registered with me, "Oh, that sounded like Cody calling me", it was gone and I must have fallen asleep because the next thing I remembered was waking up the next morning with the memory of Cody calling intact. I didn't tell anyone about it at first. I just wanted to savor the wonderful feeling of peace and happiness it brought me. And, because I wasn't sure it was real, I didn't want to tell anyone and then have them say to me, "Oh, honey, it's just your imagination. You want to hear from him so badly that you're making it happen". The same thing happened to me several nights later. I was just drifting off to sleep when, once again, sounding as if he were a long way off, I heard Cody calling, "Mom!". And once again, I had just enough time to think to myself, "That's Cody" before I dropped off to sleep. Again, I awoke the next morning with the very vivid remembrance of him calling to me just as I dropped off to sleep.

I had another similar incidence happen to me during this time frame except that I knew this was a dream. At least, part of it was a dream. I was dreaming that my daughter, Marisa, and I were at home on our hands and knees picking up books and knick-knacks from off the floor where the bookshelf had been knocked over. In the dream, we were trying to figure out how this had happened when all of a sudden, I hear the sound of footsteps running up to me and right through the pile of books on the floor along with what sounded like Cody giggling. I don't know if the sounds of the footsteps and giggling were a part of the dream or were outside of the dream. All I know is that in the dream, Marisa didn't appear to notice either of them.

Months went by and I didn't "hear" from Cody. I have to admit that I was a bit depressed. It had been so wonderful to "hear" his voice again. I know that episodes like these, visual or auditory experiences similar to hallucinations are not uncommon after the loss of a loved one. I didn't know if what I was hearing was real or not. I just knew it brought me a great deal of comfort so I didn't question it; I was just thankful for the experience, whatever it was. However, I'm not sure that what happened next can be explained away as an "auditory hallucination". It was early November and the Christmas season was just starting. Christmas was one of Cody's most favorite times of year and I was missing him more than usual. It was during this time when I was feeling down that I shared with my aunt, Cody's great-aunt who had always been open to new age phenomena, my previous experiences of "hearing" from Cody. She and Cody had had an unusually close relationship. They just seemed to "get" each other despite their age difference. I asked her if she thought Cody was really trying to contact me and, if so, why she thought it had stopped happening. I don't remember what she said but I do remember that she told me several days later that she had started meditating and talking to Cody, telling him how much I needed to hear from him and that I needed to know it for certain. Well, I do believe he listened to her!

Joni, my sister, and I were at the mall looking around, doing some Christmas shopping. It was mid-morning during the work week that first week in November so the mall wasn't very crowded. We had just stepped into a small store off the main drag of the mall when I heard him. I heard what sounded just like my Cody call "Mom" from a distance. Now, if you're a mom, you know that when you're in public, every mother within hearing distance looks up when she hears that cry. For me, time stopped at that moment. I looked around the shop and out into the mall to see if there was anyone who could be calling their mom. Not only weren't there any young people in my vicinity, not one woman, other than myself, was looking to see where the call of "Mom" had come from. I had just turned back around and hadn't even had time to digest what had just happened when the look on Joni's face stopped me in my tracks! "Did you hear that", she asked me with her face covered in disbelief? "Hear what?"I countered, not wanting to give anything away. I guess she could tell by the look on my face because she said, "You heard it, didn't you." "It sounded just like Cody calling 'Mom!'". "Yes, I heard it", I said, "I just can't believe you heard it". We both left the mall in a wonderful daze. Was this an "auditory hallucination" heard by both myself and my sister at the same time? Or, was this my Cody wanting to make sure I couldn't doubt his continued presence in my life? And was he trying to get his favorite aunt in on the deal to verify it? I don't know. But,

I wonder.

Playing With The Lights

I told you earlier about the lights flickering during the viewing the night before Cody's funeral. I've heard it said that one of the easiest ways for a deceased person's spirit to make contact with the physical world is through electricity. That certainly makes sense since we're all composed of energy. Well, one night after Marisa, Joni and I had moved into our new house, my oldest son, Matt, came over for dinner. Now, Matt had moved with his job to Tallahassee just months after Cody's death. He spent about a year there and then transferred home. Matt was very reluctant to talk about Cody and what had happened. They had been so close. In fact, all three of my children had enjoyed a good relationship with each other. It seemed easier for Marisa to talk about her feelings than it was for Matt. I think that's why I was so surprised by the experience Matt shared with us over dinner that night.

It seems that one night fairly recently Matt was lying in bed in his apartment just getting ready to go to sleep. He said he was lying on his stomach with his head propped on one arm. All of a sudden, he said a series of three blue balls of light shot through his bedroom, one after another. He said he got up to look out the window and see if by chance, there was a police car outside. There wasn't. Nor did his roommate notice anything from the living room where he was still up, watching television. Two things stood out to me as Matt was relaying this story to us. First of all, my son, who is a very logical person and not normally emotional, was very emotional as he was re-telling this event. It was obvious to me that he had experienced something which he could not logically understand and he was still visibly shaken by it. Of course the second thing that stood out was that during Matt's re-telling of the story to us, the lights in the dining room started to flicker on and off! Not just one light, but both of the lights in the room, the table lamp and the overhead fixture. We all saw them flicker and we just stared at each other and shook our heads. Remember, this was a newly built house. The overhead fixture was brand new as were the light bulbs in it and the table lamp. We did check to make sure the bulbs were screwed in tightly, and they were. Oh, and get this; they didn't flicker again after that night. And even then it was only during Matt's recounting of his previous experience with the blue balls of light.

So what are we supposed to make of this? A faulty connection that corrected itself? A figment of all of our imaginations? Or was Cody's essence, his energy there in the dining room with us that night? Was he trying to let us know he was there? And was he trying to join in the conversation? I don't know. Nor will I ever know in this life. But,

I wonder.

Coincidences?

Right around the time of the 5th anniversary of Cody's death, there was a period of time when I was missing him more than usual. I was annoyed with myself for being depressed but just couldn't seem to shake it. The day before the actual anniversary of his death, I drug myself out of bed and went into the kitchen to drink a cup of coffee and read the paper before heading out to work. As I picked up the paper one of the stories on the front page jumped out at me. It was about a young local girl who had been killed the day before in an automobile accident. She had just recently celebrated her 16th birthday. Her best friend was driving the car and survived the accident with minimal injuries. The details of the accident were very similar to those of Cody's. It made me stop and remember the pain and anguish her parent's were experiencing. It made me think of the long and arduous journey from grief to healing they were just embarking on. It made me realize how fortunate I was, I was already past that part of the journey.

I got dressed and went on into work. At the time, I was working as a licensed Realtor. Shortly after arriving at my office, I received a call from a woman who wanted me to show her a house right then, that morning. I didn't know the woman, nor did she know me. I found out afterwards that she had picked up a real estate magazine and randomly picked my name and number from an ad in the book. What makes this more interesting is that the ad wasn't for the house she wanted to see. It makes no sense, or does it? Even more interesting is the fact that I learned from her later on that had she realized I worked for the real estate company that I did, she would not have called me. She had had some less-than-positive experiences in the past with other agents in my company. After meeting the woman and driving her around to see several houses we got to talking and I learned she knew my ex-husband's parents. They had been neighbors just after we had gotten divorced. She knew all about Cody and the accident. She told me she and her husband had sent us prayers and that they both thought Charley and I had handled the situation admirably. Working with her that day helped to lift my depression. She also became a good client who both sold and bought a house through me.

Later that same day, I had yet another positive experience. I was driving back to work from an appointment when I got stopped by a funeral procession. I know, you're wondering how I interpreted getting stopped by a funeral procession as being positive. I can't explain it except to tell you that the hearse was white. Seeing that white hearse made me think it was Cody telling me he was okay, he was in Heaven and everything was alright. Strange, maybe; but all I know is it gave me a sense of well-being and comfort.

None of these things when taken individually would amount to much. Together however, they worked to ease my depression and lighten the load I found myself carrying that day. When you think about the fact that they all happened on a single day, a day when I was feeling especially down, a day just prior to the anniversary of Cody's death and at a time when I should have been doing okay but wasn't; that puts it in a different light. It had been five years since Cody's death and I had worked hard at coming to terms with my grief and had progressed to the point where I didn't usually have down days like this one. Yet here I was, right back where I started it seemed. So, did each of these events happen by luck, coincidence or random chance? Am I reading more into it than is really there? Or, did they occur by some type of Divine Intervention to help pick me up and get me back on my way? I believe everything happens for a reason and I don't believe in luck, coincidence or random chance. But,

I wonder.

Out Of The Mouth of Babes

It had been about six years since Cody's death when I was driving down the road with my precious 4-year old granddaughter, Marissa. She never knew her Uncle Cody but she had heard about him from her daddy (Matt) and mommy. There were pictures of Cody scattered about their house and many more of them in my house. So she certainly knew who he was.

My daughter Marisa (she and my granddaughter share the same name but they each spell it differently) was pregnant with her first child and we had just learned it was going to be a girl. However, little Marissa never doubted it. From the time my daughter learned she was pregnant, my granddaughter was very serious and very firm about the fact that Tia (her name for her aunt, since two Marisa's were too much for her to understand at this point in her young life) was going to have a baby <u>girl.</u> She simply wouldn't have it any other way. So, on this bright, sunny afternoon I'm in the front seat of my car with Marissa in her car seat in the back of the car and we are having a discussion about her soon to be born new cousin.

"Marissa", I said. "Tia's going to have a baby girl!" "Yep", she said. "A baby Aubrey." My daughter and son-in-law had decided on Aubrey for a girls name shortly after learning they were expecting. "You were right," I told her. "You always said it was going to be a baby girl and it is! God is giving us a beautiful baby Aubrey!" Then, from the backseat came this very quiet, calm response. "No, you gave God a beautiful baby". The words came out of Marissa's mouth but they contained nothing of her personality or her tone. Trying to stay calm, I glanced in the rear-view mirror and casually in a half-joking manner said, "I did, who"? Again, that same monotone expressionless voice came out of my granddaughter's body and said quite matter of factly, "Cody". Now you have to understand, Marissa and I hadn't been talking about Cody at all prior to this. Neither one of us had even mentioned him at all that day. Before I had time to react or to try and figure out what was happening, I once again heard my granddaughter's voice as she asked me, "Nonnie, who's Cody"? Trying to keep my wits about me and keep the car driving as if nothing was going on, I told her, "You know who Cody is. He's your uncle. He's your daddy and Tia's brother. He's in Heaven with God now." And as I heard her say in her own voice with all her personality, "I don't need another uncle, I've got Uncle Donald" (her Tia's husband and my son-in-law). I knew that whoever I had been talking to a few minutes earlier, it wasn't my granddaughter but she was most definitely back now! So, who was that in my backseat telling me I had given God a beautiful baby? I don't know. This is another one of those things I probably won't ever know in this lifetime. But,

I wonder.

Psychic Connection

I mentioned earlier that I met Sharon Renae, a wonderful psychic medium several months after Cody's death. Sharon has played a large part in helping me retain my sanity after losing Cody. I know that many of you reading this book may think just the opposite. That anyone who trusts someone purporting to communicate with the dead must be insane or a little crazy at best. Let me tell you a few things Sharon has shared with me that have helped me on my healing journey through grief.

Not too long after Matt's experience with the 'blue balls of light' my friend Brenda went on a retreat with Sharon Renae and several other people (none of whom I knew). I believe they went up to the mountains somewhere in Tennessee. After they got back home, Brenda called me and said that Sharon had gotten a message from Cody and she had asked Brenda to pass it on to me. The message was that Cody had been in touch with his brother. Now remember, there were only four (4) people who knew about Matt's experience; Matt and those of us who he told at dinner that night which would be Marisa (who to this day doesn't believe in such things as psychics and psychic phenomena), my sister Joni and me. None of us told either Brenda or Sharon Renae about the incident. Neither Matt nor Marisa knew Sharon Renae at the time. So what does this mean? Were the blue balls of light that filled Matt's bedroom some kind of message from his younger brother? Was Cody trying to get through to him? Was Sharon Renae a vessel Cody was using to help him in this effort? I don't know.

About a year ago I had a private reading with Sharon Renae. It was one of many I have had since first meeting her. Nothing of much consequence came up in this reading. At least I didn't think so at the time.

At one point in the reading Sharon said she was getting Cody's energy and he was showing her an owl. She wanted me to tell her what, if any, significance an owl would have for either Cody or me. I couldn't think of one. I told her that there was a time when Cody had worn big rimmed glasses, maybe that was what he was referring to. "No", she said. "That's not it". She wanted to know if I had a picture of an owl, had somebody given me a statue of an owl. She said she was getting a real clear picture of an owl. I couldn't think of anything that would relate to an owl so she just gave up and told me I might remember something or get the answer to the message later on. She also told me Cody had a large tabby cat with him. That didn't make any sense to me either as we never owned a cat. We were strictly a dog family.

I went home and promptly forgot about both the owl and the cat. That is until the following Saturday when I had all the family over for dinner. Now I have to regress a little bit here and tell you about my daughter and son-in-law. I think I've already mentioned Marisa, my daughter is very much against anything remotely connected to psychic phenomena. What I haven't told you is that she married a young man whose sister, Anna, died from injuries she suffered in a fatal automobile accident when she was in college. It is one of the many synchronicities that we have experienced since losing Cody. My son-in-law, Donald is his parents' only son. Marisa is my only daughter. We each had three children. Donald's parents had two girls and one boy. I had two boys and one girl. We each lost a child of the gender we had two of. Donald's parents lost one of the two daughters they had. I lost one of the two sons I had. Both died as a result of an automobile accident. Donald's mother and I each lost a brother as teenagers. On a lighter note, we both also played clarinet in our school bands. I'm telling you all of this because I believe it shows that our families are connected on a much deeper level than just the marriage of our children. Okay, back to the owl. After everyone had left that night after dinner I got a phone call from Marisa. "Mom", she said "you'll never guess what just happened to Donald and me". "What", I said. "We just had a Cody and Anna moment", she said. "What do you mean?" I asked. "We were on our way home from your house and had just turned down our road when I saw an owl sitting on the fence on the corner. I asked Donald if he had seen it and he said, no, he hadn't. I asked him to quick, back up and he did and Mom, that owl didn't move a bit. And you know how loud Donald's truck is." Donald drives a big diesel pick up truck and it is loud. "Well Mom, we backed up and I rolled my window down to get a good look at the owl and he just sat there and stared at me with his big old eyes. We finally drove away." "Wow," I said. "That's great but why did you call it a Cody and Anna moment?" "I don't know" she replied in a self-questioning tone, "I just did." "Let me ask you something," I said. "Did Anna have a cat – a tabby cat by any chance?" She said she didn't know but she asked Donald and guess what? You guessed it, seems that one of Anna's favorite pets had been a large tabby cat named Kit-Kat. So what does this mean? Is Anna in heaven with Cody? Do they know each other? Was Anna trying to get a message through to her family by communicating with me during my last session with Sharon Renae? Why an owl? Why use Marisa and Donald who don't have much use for such things? And why would they, of all people, refer to their experience as a 'Cody and Anna' moment? I don't know. Marisa and Donald live next door to my son and daughter-in-law, Matt and Sabrina and their three children. To this day, the kids tell me (and have shown me pictures to prove it) that the owl still shows up. They usually see him in the evenings when they are all outside sitting around visiting with each other. The owl will be hanging out on a power line or roof top, looking at them as if he purposely wants them to know he's there. He doesn't appear to be the least bit afraid of them or their cameras!

About five years after my initial meeting with Sharon Renae, Brenda and I took another friend of ours to a private reading with her. Even though my relationship with Sharon over the preceding years had taught me that she was an ethical woman who took her gift seriously, I remained somewhat of a skeptic. I think I was the original Doubting Thomas in another life! Anyway, I had told Sharon that I would be convinced only after she could come up with Cody's nickname for me during one of her sessions. Being the true professional she is, Sharon would admonish me not to tell her the name. Of course I wouldn't. I didn't tell Brenda or anyone else who might be in touch with Sharon Renae. Cody had a nickname for everybody. My sister Joni was Jo Jo. My parents, his grandparents were Grammy and Grampy. He reversed the B and N's in Bonnie to come up with Nobbie for me. Although I really wanted Cody to get the message of my nickname through to her, I knew it was a pretty safe bet Sharon Renae wouldn't be able to just stumble upon by accident. Prior to each visit with Sharon whether it was a group setting or a private reading, I would mentally tell Cody I was going and for him to try and get my nickname to her. I would tell him I couldn't imagine how she would get the message unless he did something like show her a doorknob. One thing that had previously shown up in my readings was baskets. All of my children knew I liked to decorate the house with baskets and we always had a bunch of them around. So getting baskets in my messages from him made sense.

On this particular visit I wasn't thinking about getting any messages myself, this visit was for my friend Theresa who had recently lost her father. Brenda and I were hoping Theresa would find some comfort in what Sharon Renae could share with her. As we get the session under way, Brenda, Theresa and I are sitting around a small table with Sharon Renae. We have our heads bent down a little bit and are holding onto each others hands. Theresa's father did seem to come through and gave her some information which she could validate. Then, at one point, I realize Theresa is starting to cry because of the strength of the messages she's getting so I start to pat her on the leg when I hear Sharon Renae say "Why is he giving me a doorknob?" I lift my head in astonishment and hear myself say, "I think that might be for me, Sharon". "I don't know who it's for", she said, "and now he's giving me a basket full of doorknobs, you know, the old antique pretty kind." "That is for me, it's my nickname!" I cried. "Doorknob"! They all chimed in unison. "Your nickname is doorknob"!? Brenda asked and they all looked at me quizzically. "No, its Nobbie" I said and explained it to them. So, it's hard to doubt after that. But,

I do wonder.

OHM

My search for Cody has enabled me to hear and see God in the minute details of everyday life. When my daughter Marisa was about three months pregnant, she started having severe pains in her left side. Prior to becoming pregnant, she had been diagnosed with Pseudotumor cerebri (PTC) which is not an uncommon problem in young women. It causes swelling of the optic nerves, resulting in severe headaches, and, if left untreated it can cause vision loss. Because pregnancy causes a woman to retain more fluid in her body, Marisa's doctor was keeping a close watch on her condition. However, this new pain she started having in her side was quickly ruled out as having anything to do with the pseudo tumor. She underwent all sorts of tests but nothing showed up. After one really bad episode with the mysterious pain and a trip to the emergency room, she was admitted to the hospital. She was there for two days and underwent quite a few more tests, all while being hooked up to IV fluids. None of the tests revealed anything that could be causing the pain in her side. Her obstetrician was at a loss as to what could be going on because everything associated with her pregnancy and the baby was okay. To make matters worse, Marisa's headaches, which had eased up, had returned with a vengeance. Everything they did was to no avail. That is, until a wonderful night nurse came to her rescue. The nurse was named Anna, just like my son-in-law's sister who had been killed in an automobile accident. Since my son-in-law's sister had died before he and Marisa met, Marisa never knew her. However, she said she felt an instant rapport with this young night nurse. She was very much at ease with her. Anna told us she didn't normally work that section of the hospital, but was pulling special duty that evening. My son-in-law is an electrician and has to be at work very early each morning. I was in real estate at the time and could pretty much set my own hours so I spent the night at the hospital with Marisa. After reviewing Marisa's chart, Anna came in the room to talk with her a bit. She asked Marisa to describe her pain and her symptoms. Marisa told Anna about the pseudo tumor and the fact that her headaches had come back along with the more pressing problem of the severe pain in her side. I noticed that Anna looked a little confused or quizzical as Marisa was talking to her. Afterwards, Anna left the room, promising to be back shortly. True to her word, she came back into the room a little while later and told Marisa, "We've got to get those fluids out of you", referring to the IV fluids the doctors had been pumping her full of. Anna had realized that with Pseudotumor cerebri, more fluids equal more swelling on the optic nerves resulting in the return of Marisa's headaches. And, as it turns out, Anna herself had just recently recovered from a bout of pneumonia and pleurisy and Marisa's symptoms sounded very much like what she had been through. She called the doctor on duty and told him of her suspicions. He arranged for Marisa to undergo an MRI.

If you don't know what an MRI unit looks like, it's a large cylinder-shaped machine which resembles a big tube. It has a moveable examination table which slides into the center of the tube where the magnet is located. The patient is instructed to lie still while in the machine. Once inside the machine, large electromagnets are rapidly switched on and off. You can't see the magnets but you can hear them. The sounds they make can be fairly loud and they differ in tone and sequence. The patient is put through a series of scans and wears headphones to help muffle the loudness of each series of tones. In between each series, the patient is conveyed back out of the machine into the room. The technician performing the test is in another room but can see the patient through a window and can communicate with them through a two-way intercom.

Though I had tried not to let Marisa know I was worried, I was. After all, here was my daughter, pregnant with her first child, experiencing severe pains that have her doctors baffled. Since it was after midnight and there were no other patients in the X-ray department, I was allowed to go in with Marisa. Since it is not common for anyone to accompany a patient into the MRI room, there were no chairs to sit on. The technician found me an uncomfortable wooden stool, which, considering the lateness of the hour and my frayed nerves was better than standing. I placed the stool beside the head of the bed so Marisa and I could talk while the technician prepared the exam. That was all fine and good until the exam started. Marisa was moved into the machine and I was left in a cold, sterile, ominously quiet hospital exam room looking at my daughter's sock covered feet. After each series of tests, the bed would slide back out and I'd have my daughter back. Prior to starting the test, the technician had asked me if I wanted a pair of headphones since the tones could be rather loud. So as Marisa disappeared into the machine for that first test, I put on the headphones and got ready. However, the headphones were tight and added to my anxiety so I took them off before the scan even got started. That first scan did startle me a bit. And while it was louder than I had thought it would be, it wasn't unbearable. The first series of magnetic tones was a short staccato sound. I honestly don't remember the next few tonal sequences, only that they were all different in sound and length. I was getting progressively more nervous each time she would disappear back into the MRI machine. After she disappeared into the MRI machine for probably the fourth or fifth time, I began to pray to God to take care of her. I knew that whatever was going on with my daughter's body, it was out of my hands. I will never forget the sound that very next tonal sequence made. Just as I am asking God to take care of my daughter, the sound I hear emanating from the MRI machine sounds exactly like the Sanskrit word, OHM which means Peace, Divine, GOD.

OHM, OHM, OHM. It filled the room and I was immediately overcome with a sense of peace and well-being. When I talked to Marisa about this later on, she said to me, "You know Mom, I know there were other sound patterns during the MRI but the OHM sound is the only one I can clearly remember".

The MRI was over shortly afterwards and Marisa and I returned to her room. A few hours later, the doctor came by to let her know that the MRI showed a pocket of pneumonia under her lung. It was situated just so that none of the other x-rays could pick it up. She was taken off the IV fluids, given some antibiotics and sent home. Her headaches subsided and she recovered fully.

Six months later she went back to the same hospital and gave birth to a wonderfully healthy baby girl, Aubrey Elizabeth. And guess who took care of the baby in the newborn nursery? You guessed it, the very same nurse, Anna. On their last night at the hospital, Aubrey, who had up to this point been a very easy baby, was very fussy. Marisa and Donald couldn't get her to calm down and neither of them was getting any rest. So Anna, who had come in to check on them after starting her shift, took her back to the nursery with her. She later told Marisa and Donald that as long as she would hold her, Aubrey was fine. So, Anna held Aubrey in her arms that last night as she made her rounds and took care of the other newborns.

Was it just a coincidence that Marisa's nurse that evening in the hospital shared some similarities to a sister-in-law she never got to know? Was it a coincidence that she was scheduled to work on a floor she didn't usually work on? Was it a coincidence that she had experienced the same symptoms Marisa had just a few months prior? And was it a coincidence that baby Aubrey would only calm down for her on their last night in the hospital? Was it a coincidence that as if in answer to a mother's prayer, I would hear the sound of God (OHM) filling the MRI room and flooding me with a peace I couldn't explain?

I wonder.

If I Could Find That Dime

Music has always been a part of our lives. When the kids were young and still depended on me to drive them around, we'd sing with the songs on the car radio. One day we were driving down the road and Cher's *If I Could Turn Back Time* came over the radio. Well, we all started singing along with her. Even Cody who was probably only four at the time was singing at the top of his little lungs. All of a sudden, Matt, Marisa and I quit singing and began laughing. It seems Cody had interpreted Cher's words to be "If I could <u>find that dime, I'd give it back to you</u>, and he was singing it proudly. Of course, he was a little offended by our laughing but we assured him we were laughing with him, not at him. After that, we all changed the words to fit Cody's interpretation and anytime we heard the song, we sang it his way. This eventually extended to most of our family and Cody became quite proud of "his song". So now, anytime we hear *If I Could Turn Back Time,* we know its Cody shouting out to us. Several years after Cody's death, his great-aunt whom he had shared a special bond with shared such an experience with me in an email. She wrote, "Well, I just got a little nudge from Cody. I went to Wendy's by myself, and as I walked in I looked around for the table that Cody and I sat at when we went there together. It's a little to the left of the center of the store – he liked the booth, and I liked my chair to face the window, which also faced him. Anyway, after I got my food and was walking to the table, I felt such a sense of sadness and loss. I asked God to help me through the sadness. At that very moment a song I had been waiting to hear, I'd never heard it before even though you all had, came over the juke box in the corner. *If I Could Turn Back Time*, If I could find that dime. My sadness lifted and I knew Cody was with me."

So, when we hear Cher's song, or should I say Cody's song, is it just a song and a coincidence? Or is it more? Is it Cody's hello from Heaven? We don't know but,

We wonder!

So, what do I make of all of this? What are you supposed to make of all this? I don't know about you, you'll have to decide for yourself. But for me, I believe. Since my Cody's accident, I've had too much happen to me and have experienced too many things which can't be explained any other way. There's more to life and to us than can be explained in our human world.

Thank God for Brenda and for our bond. Thank God for allowing her to come home and show me a different way of thinking. I truly believe that her coming home after all those years was God's way of preparing me for the journey I was about to take. A healing journey to find my Cody after he left this world. It's a journey that will take the rest of my life because I will always be open to his presence and the "visits" I get from him will allow the healing to go on forever. I don't believe you can ever completely heal from the loss of a child. But I do believe you can lessen the loss and learn to live with it by developing a different type of relationship with the child, or any loved one for that matter. I'm telling you this to let you know that I'm not a crazy, grief-stricken parent playing the victim. I'm a sane, level-headed person with my feet firmly planted on the ground. But I have made a conscious choice to look for Cody, to listen for him and to continue on with my relationship with him even though his physical body no longer exists in this world. You might read this book and come away saying, "she's crazy; she's out of touch with reality". But am I? I wonder! What this choice has really done for me is to help me retain my sanity after a time when I thought I would never be sane again. It allows me to get up out of bed every morning and continue living. Not just go through the motions, but truly live. It has given me my life back when I thought it was surely gone forever.

And that is the greatest wonder of it all.